CONFEDERATION: THE GREAT ENTERPRISE

DON QUINLAN

CANADA

A PEOPLE'S HISTORY

THOMSON

★

NELSON

Australia   Canada   Mexico   Singapore   Spain   United Kingdom   United States

THOMSON

NELSON

Canada: A People's History
Confederation: The Great Enterprise

Series Consultants
Donald Bogle, Don Quinlan

Author
Don Quinlan

Director of Publishing
Beverley Buxton

General Manager, Social Studies,
Business Studies, and Languages
Carol Stokes

Publisher, Social Studies
Doug Panasis

Managing Editor, Development
Karin Fediw

Product Manager
Nadia McIlveen

Senior Editor
Susan Petersiel Berg

Editorial Coordinator
Amy Hingston

Executive Director, Content and
Media Production
Renate McCloy

Director, Content and Media
Production
Lisa Dimson

Production Manager
Cathy Deak

Senior Production Coordinator
Kathrine Pummell

Interior and Cover Design
Daniel Crack, Kinetics Design

Photo Research
Lisa Brant, Alene McNeill

Printer
Transcontinental Printing Inc.

Canadian Broadcasting
Corporation Representative
Karen Bower

The authors and the publisher are
grateful to the Canadian
Broadcasting Corporation for its
assistance in the preparation of
this volume in the book series
based on its 17-episode, bilingual
television documentary series,
Canada: A People's History. For
more information about *Canada:*
A People's History, please visit
www.cbc.ca/history.

Canada: A People's History
© 2000, 2001 Canadian
Broadcasting Corporation

Contents

THE BIG IDEA

Until 1867, there was no nation called Canada. Instead, there was a string of small British colonies—separated by forests, plains, and mountains—that spread across the northern part of the continent. Canada began with the union of four of these colonies: New Brunswick, Nova Scotia, Canada East (now Quebec), and Canada West (now Ontario). They formed the core of a nation that quickly grew to become the second biggest country in the world, one of the richest nations in history, and home to people from around the globe.

At the London Conference in 1866, delegates from the British North American colonies worked out the final details for the new Dominion of Canada. How would you describe these delegates?

TIMELINE

1847 Irish Potato Famine: Irish immigrants pour into the colonies

1861 American Civil War begins

1840 Act of Union creates United Province of Canada (Canada West and Canada East)

1854 Reciprocity Treaty sets up free trade between British North America colonies and U.S.

1. Hewitt Bernard, secrétaire
2. W.H. Steeves
3. Edward Whelan
4. W.H. Henry
5. Charles Fisher
6. J.H. Gray, Î.-P.-É.
7. Edward Palmer
8. G.H. Coles
9. S.L. Tilley
10. F.B.T. Coles
11. Jean-Charles Chapais
12. J.A. Shea
13. E.B. Chandler
14. Alexander Campbell
15. A.G. Archibald
16. Hector-Louis Langevin
17. John A. Macdonald
18. George-Étienne Cartier
19. Sir Étienne-Paschal Taché

20. George Brown
21. T.H. Haviland
22. A.T. Galt
23. Peter Mitchell
24. James Cockburn
25. Oliver Mowat
26. R.B. Dickey
27. Charles Tupper
28. J.H. Gray, N.-B.
29. W.H. Pope
30. William McDougall
31. Thomas D'Arcy McGee
32. A.A. Macdonald
33. Jonathan McCully
34. J.M. Johnson
35. R.D. Wilmot
36. W.P. Howland
37. J.W. Ritchie

TIMELINE

Sir John A. Macdonald

1864 September: Charlottetown Conference

October: Quebec Conference drafts 72 Resolutions

1865 American Civil War ends

1866 London Conference drafts British North America Act

End of Reciprocity Treaty with U.S.

Fenians invade Canada

1867 Birth of the Dominion of Canada

Sir John A. Macdonald becomes Canada's first prime minister

PICTURE THIS

How are countries made? How did Canada become a country? Why is there still a Canada? Will it last forever? Do Canadians today have any say about the nature of their country? Can they change it in any way? These are difficult and demanding questions. Consider them carefully as you learn about the birth of Canada.

SETTING THE SCENE

The colonies of British North America (BNA) did not have to unite. In fact, many colonists thought they should remain separate. They were proud of their British or French heritage and doubtful about the benefits of a union. Others wanted to see the colonies unite but continue to be part of the powerful empire headed by Britain. There were also people in the colonies who thought that, sooner or later, Canada would join the young, strong country to the south, the United States of America. Certainly many Americans believed it was only a matter of time before all of North America would be flying the U.S. flag. Few people imagined the British colonies becoming a new nation.

Robert Harris's painting of the Fathers of Confederation (at left) shows the middle window larger than it really was so that the focus falls on the central figure of Sir John A. Macdonald, Canada's first prime minister. The painting was destroyed in a fire that burned down the Parliament Buildings in 1916. The men portrayed in this painting are usually given credit for making Confederation happen. As you read about Confederation, think about who you believe are the most important people in the story.

CHANGE AND CONFLICT

The colonists in British North America and the people of the United States had different approaches to change. The United States was born in 1776, following the **American Revolution**. By 1861, the country was caught up in the brutal and bloody Civil War. This war between the northern and southern states lasted five years and killed 600 000 people. For Americans, the changes involved in nation building were full of violence and conflict.

The colonists of British North America preferred a process of gradual change—a process of evolution rather than revolution. Although the colonies had experienced rebellions against the governments of Upper and Lower Canada in 1837, they had been far less violent than the wars in the U.S.

The American Civil War raged for five years, from 1861 to 1865, with mounting death and destruction. At times, the violence threatened to sweep across the border into the colonies of British North America. Avoiding the violence and bloodshed of the American Civil War became a major concern for people hoping to build a nation from the scattered colonies of British North America.

NATION BUILDING

Nation building does not simply happen on its own. It is a process that begins with people demanding change, and usually involves strong leaders. Who would lead the creation of a Canadian nation? Would the decision to become a country be a popular idea supported by most of the people, or an unpopular one forced on the colonies by men of power and influence? Would the colonies follow the American example and build a nation through war and violence? Or could they work together in a spirit of peace and cooperation?

In 1837, a small band of rebels, led by William Lyon Mackenzie, marched to Toronto in an attempt to overthrow the government of Upper Canada. Disorganized and poorly armed, the rebel forces were quickly defeated.

Why Think About Nation Building?

Why does it matter how Canada became a nation 140 years ago? Does the union of four tiny colonies in 1867 mean anything to Canadians today? Does **Confederation** give you any special rights or responsibilities? Is our nation building finished?

As you examine the story of Confederation, think about some of these questions.

Canadians today live in a peaceful country that is one of the world's richest nations. How often do they think about the roots of their fortunate nation? Do Canadians have any special loyalty or responsibility to their country?

From Canada's history, you might get some new ideas. One day, you may have an opportunity to participate in the ongoing nation building and history of Confederation and Canada.

◀ Playback ▶

1. Which colonies united to form Canada in 1867?

2. What choices other than Confederation did the colonies have?

3. How did Canadians and Americans differ in their approach to change?

4. How different do you think Americans and Canadians are today? Explain.

5. Is it important to you to know about the origins of Canada? Why or why not?

CHAPTER I

BRITISH NORTH AMERICA IN THE 1860S

Arctic Ocean

RUSSIAN TERRITORY (ALASKA)

NORTH-WESTERN TERRITORY

NEWFOUNDLAND

Hudson Bay

Pacific Ocean

BRITISH COLUMBIA

RUPERT'S LAND

St. John's

VANCOUVER ISLAND

Victoria

CANADA EAST

PRINCE EDWARD ISLAND

Charlottetown

RED RIVER SETTLEMENT

Halifax

Quebec City

Saint NOVA

Montreal

John SCOTIA

CANADA

NEW

Ottawa

BRUNSWICK

Atlantic Ocean

Scale

WEST

0   500 km

UNITED   STATES

Toronto

FROM SEA TO SEA TO SEA

In the mid-1800s, the scattered colonies of British North America had little in common other than a fear of being taken over by the United States and a tie to far-off Britain. Each colony was led by a governor who represented the British Crown. By 1860, the British connection was getting weaker. The distant colonies were expensive to support and difficult to defend. Britain was starting to think that the time had come for the colonies to look after themselves.

In the 1860s, British North America was thinly populated with far-flung colonies that stretched from the Atlantic to the Pacific to the Arctic. In 1867, Confederation joined New Brunswick, Nova Scotia, Canada East, and Canada West. There was much growing and nation building to be done before Canada could take the form that it has today.

First Nations people had
lived for thousands of years
in most parts of Canada.
Many played an important
role in its early exploration,
settlement, and economic
development. In the 1860s,
Aboriginal trappers in the
North-Western Territory
were essential to the
success of the fur trade.

THE LAND AND ITS PEOPLE

In the middle of the nineteenth century, British North
America was a vast landscape of forests, plains, lakes,
mountains, and rivers that separated a handful of cities and
settlements. On the west coast were the tiny colonies of
Vancouver and Victoria. The mountain ranges and plains
of the huge North-Western Territory were home to
Aboriginal and **Métis** communities and a few fur-trading
posts. The Hudson's Bay Company operated its fur-trading
business on land it owned in what is now northern Ontario
and Quebec. The colony with the biggest population, the
most farmers, and the largest towns was the United Province
of Canada. It was made up of Canada West, which was
mostly English and Protestant, and Canada East, which
was mostly French and Catholic. To the east were the four
Atlantic colonies: New Brunswick, Nova Scotia, Prince
Edward Island, and Newfoundland. What would it take
to turn this string of colonies spread across an immense
territory into a nation?

First Nations

In the 1860s, about 100 000 First Nations people from
many groups lived in British North America. Most lived in
the West, where there were few settlers to interfere with

their traditional way of life. In the eastern colonies, war, disease, and the arrival of white settlers had devastated Aboriginal communities; by 1860, only 20 000 Aboriginal people were left. Some tried to farm on the reserves the government had given them in exchange for their land rights. Others moved far to the north and west to live as hunters and trappers.

French Descendants

More than 1 000 000 people lived in Canada East. The majority were French Catholic descendants of the first settlers whose families had lived in the New World for generations. They resented the small but powerful English Protestant community that ran the banks and railways, owned the leading businesses, and lived in Montreal's wealthy neighbourhoods. There were also French-speaking descendants of Acadians in Nova Scotia and New Brunswick.

British Immigrants

British immigrants made up most of the population in the Atlantic colonies, in Canada West, and in the settlements on the west coast. During the 1800s, thousands of poor farmers and factory workers from England, Scotland, Ireland, and Wales arrived in British North America looking for a new life. They settled among the Loyalists, who had moved from the United States to British North America during the American Revolution.

In the 1860s, Montreal was a prosperous city, but there were divisions brewing between the French Catholic and the English Protestant communities.

By the 1860s, Halifax was a busy port with close ties to Britain.

The Industrial Revolution brought machines and factories to the cities of Britain. Shoes, furniture, and cloth—once made by hand in hundreds of small village shops—were produced by machines in factories. Huge clouds of black smoke from factory chimneys hung over the cities.

COMING TO CANADA

Most people who immigrated to the colonies in the 1800s were fleeing from desperate circumstances at home. British factory workers and Irish tenant farmers immigrated to escape poverty and starvation. Black slaves from the southern United States escaped to the colonies to live as free men and women.

Escaping Starvation

During the Industrial Revolution in Britain, poor country people flocked to the cities to work in factories. The jobs were dangerous, the hours were long, and the pay was low. Workers living in overcrowded slums dreamed of immigrating to British North America, where they could buy their own farms. The British government, concerned about its overcrowded cities, offered people cheap fares on ships travelling to the colonies.

Of all the people who left Britain to escape poverty, the Irish were the largest group. In 1847, when potato crops across the country turned black and rotted in the fields, one million people died of starvation in what came to be known as the Irish Potato Famine. Another million people boarded ships bound for North America.

When potato crops failed in Ireland in the 1840s, landlords forced tenant farmers off of the land and out of their homes. Many families wandered the countryside begging for food, sometimes eating grass to survive.

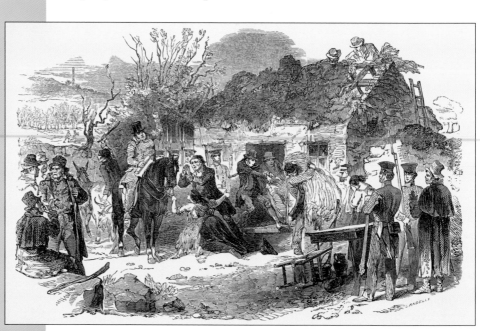

NEL

Coffin Ships at Grosse Île

On board the ships, passengers already weak from hunger were crowded together in filthy conditions. Soon typhus, smallpox, diphtheria, and cholera were spreading from one passenger to another. One eyewitness wrote: "Hundreds of people—men, women and children of all ages—huddle together. They have no fresh air. They wallow in filth. They are often sick. People with the fever lie among the healthy. They can get no food or medicine, except what other passengers can give them. They die without spiritual guidance." So many people died on board that the ships were called "coffin ships."

To keep the deadly diseases out of the colonies, officials quarantined the new immigrants at Grosse Île, an island in the St. Lawrence River near Quebec City. Thousands died, and the only mark they made on the land was a ragged line of crosses marking their graves. In 1847, 398 ships landed at Grosse Île. Of 100 000 desperate Irish immigrants who dreamed of a new life in the colonies of British North America, 5000 died at sea and more than 5000 died at Grosse Île.

Days of Sorrow

"Far from their own beloved isle
Those Irish exiles sleep;
They lie—old Ireland's exiled dead,
In cross-crowned lonely grave."

— THOMAS O'HAGAN, GROSSE ISLE

Immigrants disembarking from the coffin ships at Grosse Île were quarantined before they were allowed to start new lives in the colonies.

Telling Their Stories

JANE SLOCOMBE AND THE GREY NUNS

Watch *Canada: A People's History*, Episode 8: The Great Enterprise, "A Winter of Utter Misery" (0:42:47 to 0:47:54). Write a diary entry in role as Jane Slocombe describing the reasons why the Grey Nuns felt the need to help people in their city.

Escaping Slavery

Although slavery was outlawed across the British Empire in 1834, it remained legal in the United States. Black slaves were considered property, just like horses and furniture. Most were treated brutally. Some were murdered. Many dreamed of freedom in the slave-free colonies of British North America, especially in Canada West. Between 1840 and 1860, thousands of slaves escaped to British North America, most via the "Underground Railroad."

The Underground Railroad

The Underground Railroad was not an actual railroad. It was a secret network of Canadians and Americans who helped Black slaves escape to British North America or the northern United States. The "railway stations" were safe houses where they stayed on their journey north. The "conductors" were people who gave them food and a place to hide. Before slavery was abolished in the U.S. in 1865 following the American Civil War, 34 000 slaves had escaped to freedom in British North America, doubling its Black population.

"Farewell old master,
That's enough for me,
I'm going straight to Canada
Where coloured men are free."

The Underground Railway delivered slaves to "terminals" along the border between the U.S. and the colonies—places like Windsor, Amherstburg, Saint John, Toronto, and Montreal.

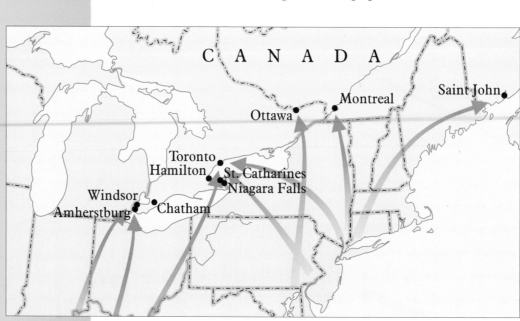

Black Heroes
Mary Ann Shadd

Mary Ann Shadd, born a free Black in the U.S., immigrated to Canada in 1851. She opened the first school where both Black and white students were educated together. The first woman in the colonies to run a newspaper, the *Provincial Freeman*, she wrote about the abolition of slavery and gave a voice to Black refugees. Mary Ann returned to the U.S. to help recruit Black soldiers to fight against slavery in the Civil War.

Josiah Henson

Born into slavery, Josiah Henson escaped to Canada West in 1830. He became an Underground Railway conductor and helped 118 slaves escape to freedom. In 1842, he moved to Chatham and established the community of Dawn, where former slaves ran their own schools, mills, and church. Josiah Henson is thought to have been the model for the character of Uncle Tom in Harriet Beecher Stowe's book, *Uncle Tom's Cabin*.

Harriet Tubman: The Black Moses

As a slave, Harriet Tubman endured terrible beatings before she escaped. In 1851, she arrived in St. Catharines in Canada West. She was so successful leading slaves to freedom that slave owners offered a reward for her capture. While the American Civil War was raging, Harriet worked as a spy and scout. When slavery was abolished at the end of the war, she became an activist in the U.S.

**Mary Ann Shadd
Born: Wilmington, Delaware, 1823
Died: Washington, D.C., 1893**

**Josiah Henson
Born: Charles County, Maryland, 1789
Died: Dresden, Ontario, 1883**

**Harriet Tubman
Born: Dorchester, Maryland, 1820
Died: Auburn, New York, 1913**

◄ Playback ►

1. Briefly describe British North America in the 1860s.

2. Who were the main groups of people who made up the population of British North America in the 1860s?

3. If you had been alive in the 1800s, would you have become involved in the activities of the Underground Railroad? Explain.

THE NEW SOCIETY AND ECONOMY

The **Industrial Revolution** came to British North America in the 1850s. By the 1860s, new factories in the largest cities were producing farm machinery, carriages, shoes, beer, sails, and rope. Railways had been built to move passengers and goods. Telegraph lines improved communication between major towns. For the wealthy, new machines and technology brought more prosperity. For the poor, who laboured on farms or moved to the cities to find jobs in the harbours and factories, life in the colonies meant hard work for low pay.

Newfoundland

The people in this colony of 122 000 lived in the bustling port of St. John's or in tiny fishing outports sprinkled along the windswept coast. Newfoundland was the most British of the North American colonies. Facing the Atlantic Ocean and isolated from its neighbours, the colony felt closer to London than to Montreal or Toronto. The main industries were fishing and seal hunting. Poor soil for farming, a harsh climate, and unpredictable fish stocks led to many hard years. By the time of Confederation, Newfoundlanders had endured several seasons of bad fishing and harsh poverty.

Fishing off the coast of Newfoundland, mid-1800s

Prince Edward Island

The smallest in population (94 000) and size, Prince Edward Island was a colony of farmers and fishers. The Islanders were independent and hard working, and resented the power of the wealthy landlords who owned their land but lived far away in Britain.

British landlords owned most of the farmland in P.E.I.

Ship building in Nova Scotia, 1860s

Nova Scotia

Nova Scotia was so prosperous that some people called the 1860s a Golden Age for this colony of 400 000. It had the timber and the shipwrights to support a thriving ship-building industry. Fishing and lumbering flourished. Nova Scotia exported coal, fish, and wood to hungry markets in the United States. The British navy used Halifax as a naval port, and a new railway from Truro to Halifax promised future wealth.

The forests in New Brunswick were rapidly cut down to supply wood for building ships and new communities. Conservation was not a concern in the 1860s.

New Brunswick

New Brunswick was a lively colony with rich forests, many rivers, and a year-round, ice-free harbour. Its main industry was logging, and its people exported high-quality wood for ship masts and building lumber to the United States and Britain. Saint John was one of the largest towns in British North America. A railway promised the start of a new age for its population of nearly 300 000.

United Province of Canada

In 1841, the British government united Upper and Lower Canada to create the United Province of Canada. The growing colony was dynamic but divided. The mainly English-speaking and Protestant people of Canada West were uncomfortable being tied to the French-speaking and Catholic people of Canada East.

Canada West was almost bursting at the seams with a rapidly growing population of 1 525 000. Most of the good farmland had already been claimed. Settlers had cleared forests, built roads, and established towns and villages. Hungry for more land and power, farmers, business owners, and political leaders eagerly eyed the vast lands to the west owned by the Hudson's Bay Company. Railway mania had business people dreaming of shipping crops, lumber, and factory-made goods across the land.

The bustling town of London in Canada West

This image of life in Canada East in the mid-1800s suggests many things about how people lived and played at the time. What winter activities can you find?

Canada East was Canada West's sister colony but had different ambitions. The population was smaller (1 112 000) and mainly French and Catholic. Unlike the Protestants of Canada West who favoured a non-religious education system, the people of Canada East believed strongly in Catholic schools. They distrusted Canada West and the English merchants who dominated Montreal and Quebec City. Afraid of being outnumbered by new English settlers, few yearned to take over the western territories. Canada East and West may have been provincial partners, but by the 1860s, the cracks in their union were showing.

Rupert's Land, 1850s

Rupert's Land

A land of plains and mountains, **Rupert's Land** was owned by the Hudson's Bay Company. It was home to Aboriginal communities and a string of remote fur-trading posts. Red River, a farming and fur-trading community of 13 000 Métis and a few thousand white settlers, was the only large settlement in Rupert's Land. Would the territory be swallowed by the U.S., or unite with the scattered British North American colonies?

British Columbia

The tiny settlements on the west coast were closer to the American states and to Russian-owned Alaska than to any of the British North American colonies. Until 1856, only 1000 white immigrants lived in a region that was home to 50 000 Aboriginal people belonging to dozens of nations. The Gold Rush of 1858 drew hordes of American fortune hunters to the area. By the time they left, the Aboriginal population, devastated by disease, had dropped to 30 000, and the white community had grown to 10 000. Many people believed that the U.S. would absorb the isolated coastal colonies.

A First Nations village on the B.C. coast, 1850s

THE CHALLENGE

The dream of uniting the British North American colonies had been proposed as early as 1858. However, even attempts to connect them by rail had been too difficult because of a rugged landscape. Each colony had its own territory and its own government, and even its own postage stamps. Some believed it was only a matter of time before the colonies fell one by one into the hands of the United States. There was little pulling the colonies together. Proud of their freedom and traditions, yet suspicious of each other, the colonies needed to be pushed into Confederation. The deal making and nation building of the "Great Enterprise" was about to begin.

Canada's First Confederation

1867 was not the year of the first successful confederation in Canadian history. Nor was Sir John A. Macdonald the first father of a confederation. It was Dekanahwideh, the Aboriginal leader who in 1570 led five Iroquois nations—Mohawk, Seneca, Oneida, Onondaga, and Cayuga—into a powerful union. When the Tuscarora joined in 1715, the Iroquois Confederacy became the Six Nations.

Dekanahwideh provided a constitution, called the Great Law of Peace, to guide the Iroquois in their future relationships. Women had a more powerful and active role in this confederation than in the confederation that created the Dominion of Canada.

◀ Playback ▶

1. Carefully complete a chart of the different colonies and territories in British North America in the 1860s using the following headings. Be sure to leave enough room for your notes and additional notes from classroom discussion.

Name of Colony or Territory	Location	Approximate Population in 1860s	Economy	Your Impressions

2. In which colony would you have preferred to live? Why?

3. How was technology changing life in the colonies? Be specific.

4. What are the most important technological changes affecting Canadians today?

5. Briefly summarize the main challenge facing British North America in the mid-1860s.

The Back Story

Generations of Canadians have endured difficulty and danger when coming to Canadian shores. These include the Irish in the 1840s, the Ukrainians in the late nineteenth century, the Vietnamese and Tamils in the twentieth century, and Black slaves escaping to freedom in the 1840s to the 1860s.

The Goal

Working in groups of three or four, create a portfolio that presents a range of documents about the history of the people involved in the Underground Railroad.

The Steps

1. Decide on the items for your portfolio. Include at least 10 different items; half should be written text. Consider original or copied illustrations, real or imagined quotations, speeches and diary items, maps, mini-biographies of important figures, imagined interviews with escaped slaves, and original or re-created eyewitness accounts.

2. Research your portfolio using resources from the library, the Internet, community groups, and so on. Web sites for Library and Archives Canada, the Government of Canada's Digital Collections, and the United States National Park Service all include information and documents about the Underground Railroad.

3. To prepare your portfolio, assign each group member responsibility for some items, as discussed in your group.

4. Prepare a rough draft or sketch of each item in your portfolio. Complete a final draft after getting reactions and comments from your peers and/or your teacher.

5. Create a table of contents.

6. Title your portfolio and present it to your classmates.

History in Action

The Underground Railroad Portfolio

Evaluating Your Work

As you work, keep these criteria in mind. Be sure to:

- refer to the steps above to ensure that you have followed instructions
- review each piece with your group members for suggestions and reactions
- make sure that your portfolio package is complete and well designed
- use your imagination to re-create the past.

CHAPTER 2

COLONIES IN CRISIS

The 1860s were troubled times for British North America. Political, social, military, and economic problems threatened to overwhelm the colonies. Britain was reluctant to continue defending its distant outposts, but British North America was too big for the colonies to defend themselves. Constant disagreements between the representatives of Canada West and Canada East in the Legislative Assembly of the United Province of Canada had brought decision making to a standstill. In Canada West, early settlers had already claimed the best farmland, and there was not much left for new immigrants. Some colonists wanted to expand the colony into the vast plains of Rupert's Land. So did the United States.

Over the years, some politicians had suggested that the colonies unite, but to most people, it was a distant, unrealistic dream. The idea of Confederation was a tricky jigsaw puzzle with many hard-to-fit pieces.

RAILWAY MANIA

To the politicians and business people of Canada West, Rupert's Land seemed empty, even though it was home to thousands of Aboriginal people and Métis. They imagined waves of new settlers immigrating, starting farms, building communities, and buying goods made in their factories. If Canada West took over the territory, it would gain power and wealth. If Rupert's Land fell to the Americans, the colonies would be more isolated from each other than they already were.

Everyone knew that opening the West would be impossible without good transportation to move people, grain, livestock, and manufactured goods from the colonies in the east to new settlements in Rupert's Land. The colonists had already seen the frightening problems of a poor transportation system. In 1861, Britain had sent 14 000 soldiers to protect Canada West from the threat of an American attack. When their ship reached the St. Lawrence River, the water had started to freeze, and the soldiers were forced to march 1100 kilometres overland in deep snow. Railways seemed to be the modern answer. In this era of "railway mania," people thought of trains as wonderful engines of progress and success.

Canada's first railway, completed in 1836, was the Champlain–Saint Lawrence Railway. The first international line in the world, the St. Lawrence and Atlantic Railway, linked towns in Canada East with Portland, Maine. The Grand Trunk Railroad, stretching from Sarnia to Quebec City, was one of the longest systems in the world. In 1853, Canada built its first locomotive. By 1860, the Canadian colonies had over 350 kilometres of track.

Railway building was expensive. At one point, the Grand Trunk Railway had to pay for 1400 people and 2000 horses to clear land, build bridges, and lay track. Railway companies were losing money because it cost them

Train Wreck!

Canada's first train wreck occurred near what is now Hamilton, Ontario in 1854 when the Des Jardines Canal bridge collapsed, dropping the passing train into the frozen water below. Sixty people died. Canada's worst train disaster was in 1864, when a passenger train, the "Immigrant Special," approached a wooden swing bridge over the Richelieu River. The bridge was still open and the train hurtled into the water. Nearly 100 people, mostly new immigrants, were killed. Whole families died, ending their dreams of a bright future in British North America.

more to run the trains than they earned from passenger tickets and freight fees. Colonial legislatures and British investors had to keep bailing out the railroads.

Business people hoped that uniting the colonies would lead to new, longer railways built with government money. Some colonists thought that the railway promoters were greedy and interested only in profit, but they also realized that more railways were needed to connect the colonies, improve trade, strengthen defence, and speed up settlement.

THE ECONOMY

The economy of the colonies was dependent on selling raw materials—mostly lumber, grain, and fish—to other countries. Until the mid-1800s, their major trading partner was Britain, which imposed lower **tariffs** on imports from all its colonies. This special arrangement ended in 1846. Britain decided to begin trading with the rest of the world, and British North America lost its best customer.

In 1854, the colonies signed a reciprocity, or free-trade, agreement, with the United States—the only market big enough to replace Britain. The colonies found American buyers for their goods and dreamed of a bright economic future.

By the mid-1860s, however, economic uncertainty had returned. In 1865, the United States ended its free-trade agreement with the colonies. The small, isolated colonies were drowning in debt, and some people began to think that the only solution was a union that fostered trade among the colonies.

◄ Playback ►

1. **Briefly describe the major transportation problem facing British North America in the 1860s. Why was this problem so important?**

2. **What were the advantages and disadvantages of "railway mania"?**

3. **Assume you lived in British North America during the 1860s. Write a one-page letter to a friend outlining your concerns about the future. Describe some of the problems and suggest your own solutions.**

"The United States have frightful numbers of soldiers and guns. They wanted Florida and seized it. They wanted Louisiana and purchased it. They wanted Texas and stole it. Then they picked a quarrel with Mexico and got California. If we had not the strong arm of England over us, we too would be part of the states."

—D'Arcy McGee,
member of the Legislative Assembly
of the Province of Canada

In John Gast's painting, *American Progress*, an angelic woman who symbolizes the U.S. leads settlers to the American West.

THREATS OUTSIDE

In the 1860s, the colonies faced problems other than economic ones. As the guns of the American Civil War began to fall silent, the colonies also had reasons to fear a military threat from the U.S.

During the Civil War, Britain supported the **Confederate** forces in the southern states. Their enemies on the **Union** side in the northern states were well armed with guns and soldiers, and might seek revenge against Britain by invading its colonies at the end of the war. If the powerful forces of the Union Army attacked, the colonies feared that Britain would be slow to defend them because of the heavy costs of sending its soldiers so far from home.

Another American threat was hanging over the colonies. Many Americans thought it was God's plan that all of North America should belong to the United States, a belief called "**Manifest Destiny**." They already had their eyes on Rupert's Land. If the colonies had any hope of expanding west, they had to act fast.

DIVISIONS INSIDE

Just as dangerous to the future of British North Americans were their own internal divisions. Wide gaps in living standards separated the rich and the poor. Farmers and lumbermen in the countryside felt little connection with the wealthy merchants and railway promoters in Toronto, Montreal, Halifax, and Saint John. The people of Newfoundland had nothing in common with the people in Canada West. There was conflict between French Catholics in Canada East and English Protestants in Canada West.

POLITICAL STALEMATE

Since their union in 1841, Canada West and Canada East had lived uncomfortably together. The politicians of Canada West enthusiastically promoted canals, railroads, and factories. The leaders of Canada East were most concerned about protecting the French language, culture, and Catholic faith. Canada West wanted to take over Rupert's Land and bring in new settlers. Canada East was afraid that, with thousands of new British immigrants, the English would greatly outnumber the French.

To make sure they had an equal say in government decisions, Canada East and Canada West each had the same number of seats in the Legislative Assembly. At first, the people of Canada East outnumbered the people of Canada West. That soon changed as thousands of Irish immigrants escaping from the Potato Famine poured into Canada West. Leaders in Canada West argued that the English part of the colony should have more representatives in government. Leaders in Canada East scoffed at the idea, pointing out that the French part of the colony had not been offered more representatives when its population was the larger one.

With so much conflict, government members couldn't agree on anything. Decision making was slowing to a halt.

George-Étienne Cartier

"*I believe in the sincerity of John A. Macdonald … It is lucky indeed that two men should meet—who are in such perfect agreement over how to govern a United Province of Canada.*"

Sir John A. Macdonald

"*If we wish to be a great people, if we wish to form a great nationality, commanding the respect of the world, able to hold our own against all opponents … this can only be obtained by union.*"

THE GREAT COALITION

A way out of the mess came from a surprising source. George Brown was a Toronto newspaper editor and a leader in Canada West. For months, he had been criticizing the leading government partners, John A. Macdonald and George-Étienne Cartier, in the pages of his newspaper, *The Globe*. He accused Canada East of forcing its wishes on Canada West. He campaigned loudly for representation by population.

To get the government back to the work of running the colony, Brown went to Macdonald and Cartier, his political enemies, with a remarkable offer. He would agree to work with them as partners, if they would agree to pursue Confederation. In a confederation, each colony would have its own government to make decisions about local concerns, such as education, but the colonies would also unite in a national government to share responsibility for big projects, such as an army, railways, and trade with other countries.

George Brown

"*For ten years I have stood opposed to the honourable gentlemen opposite … But I think the House will admit that, if a crisis has ever arisen in the political affairs of any country that would justify such a coalition, such a crisis has now arrived in the history of Canada.*"

Government members from both Canada East and West were so relieved they might finally get past their stalemate that they crowded around to embrace Brown and shake his hand. One representative from Canada East rushed across the floor and leaped into the arms of the man who just the day before had been a political enemy.

The three political leaders overcame personal and cultural differences to unite in a gamble that the future of British North America lay in a confederation.

The trio—George Brown, John A. Macdonald, and George-Étienne Cartier—formed the "Great Coalition."

Now that Canada East and Canada West had agreed to a confederation, it was time to convince the rest of the colonies to join them.

Telling Their Stories

GEORGE-ÉTIENNE CARTIER

Watch *Canada: A People's History*, Episode 8: The Great Enterprise, "I Am a French Canadian" (0:09:10 to 0:14:54). Write a character sketch of George-Étienne Cartier. What qualities do you think made him popular with the people? What qualities do you think may have caused problems for him?

"The Prophet of Confederation"
Thomas D'Arcy McGee

Born: Carlingford, Ireland, 1825
Died: Ottawa, Canada, 1868

ONE of the millions of Irish who immigrated to North America was Thomas D'Arcy McGee, a man who became the most eloquent spokesman in favour of Confederation. He spent years in the United States as a newspaper editor and activist against British rule over Ireland. He moved to Canada in 1857 to edit a newspaper called the *New Era*. In 1858 he was elected in Montreal to represent Canada East and quickly established himself as a brilliant, passionate speaker. He became part of the Great Coalition, arguing for Confederation and the dream of establishing a "new nationality" from coast to coast.

◄ Playback ►

1. **What evidence was there that the Americans were a serious military threat to the inhabitants of British North America?**

2. **Briefly explain the reasons for the divisions between Canada West and Canada East.**

3. **What are the major problems facing Canada today? In your view, which is most important? Why?**

The Back Story

In the 1860s, British North America faced issues of all kinds—political, military, economic, and social. How would the colonies solve the puzzle of how to move forward as a nation?

The Goal

Working in small groups, consider the following list of problems and offer some solutions. Be sure to suggest how a union of the colonies might help or hinder the problems.

The Steps

1. Copy the organizer below into your notebook.
2. Fully discuss the impact Confederation might have on each of the problems before completing the organizer.
3. Be prepared to share your findings with your classmates.

History in Action

Solving the Jigsaw

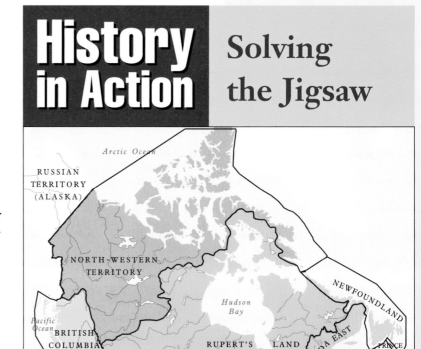

Problem	Why It Is Important	How Confederation Might Help	How Confederation Might Not Help	Our Final View and Why
The Land				
The People				
Railway Building				
The Economy				
U.S. Military Threat				
Political Divisions				

Evaluating Your Work

As you work, keep these criteria in mind. Be sure to:
• base your work on careful review of your text and notes
• participate in analysis and discussion with your group
• complete the chart carefully and neatly.

CHAPTER 3

BUILDING A NATION

The United States fought its battle for nationhood with guns and cannons. Canada fought a war of words. Written words. Spoken words. French and English words. Calm words and passionate words. In a few hurried weeks in 1864, delegates representing five colonies built the skeleton of the country's constitution. Remarkably, the agreement is virtually the same one that governs Canada today, over 140 years later.

In 1864, the colonies sent delegates to a conference in Charlottetown. It was the first step on the road to Confederation.

This famous painting shows William H. Pope rowing into the Charlottetown harbour to greet the delegates from Canada. Actually, Pope did not do all the work himself. He found a fisherman to row him out. The first meeting of the people who shaped Confederation took place not in a stately hall, but in a boat smelling of fish and oysters. Why do you suppose the fisherman has been removed from the painting? What does this suggest to you about using images to study historical events?

CHARLOTTETOWN: THE FIRST STEP

September 1–7, 1864

In the first week of September 1864, 15 **Maritimers** and 8 Canadians met in Charlottetown, Prince Edward Island, and laid the foundation of an historic agreement. The sky was clear, the weather warm, and the whole town of 7000 was captivated by the famous Slaymaker and Nichol's Olympic Circus, which was visiting the island for the first time in 20 years. Few people realized that outside the circus tent, politicians would soon be performing their own high-wire act.

Maritime leaders had planned a Charlottetown meeting to talk about uniting Nova Scotia, New Brunswick, and Prince Edward Island. (Newfoundland, tied more closely to Britain, did not attend.) The Canadians, buoyed

by their own thoughts of a union, asked if they could sit in the meeting to hear the discussions.

The key leaders from Canada East and West sailed into the harbour on the steamship *Victoria*, eager to talk and ready to celebrate with $13 000 worth of champagne stored in the ship's hold. With the whole town mesmerized by the circus, no one noticed their arrival. Eventually, one Maritime representative, William Pope, grabbed a small boat and rowed out to greet the dignitaries.

Getting Down to Business

When the Charlottetown meeting opened, the leaders of Nova Scotia, New Brunswick, and Prince Edward Island quickly agreed to set aside the subject of a Maritime union until they heard what the Canadians had to say.

The Canadians had done a lot of thinking and studying since George Brown, John A. Macdonald, and George-Étienne Cartier formed their coalition. They took to the floor with energy and conviction. Macdonald introduced the idea of uniting the colonies. Brown described the way the new provinces would share power. Alexander Galt, backed by pages of calculations, explained how a confederation would manage finances. The Maritime delegates were genuinely interested and asked many questions. One P.E.I. delegate wrote: "The Canadians descended among us, and before they were three days among us, we forgot our own scheme and thought only about theirs."

When it was all over, plans for a Maritime union had been forgotten, and thoughts of a confederation—"if terms of union could be made satisfactory"—had taken centre stage. The leaders agreed to meet again in a month in Quebec to hammer out the details. Few of the merry delegates realized how much hard work lay ahead.

This photo of the Fathers of Confederation at the Charlottetown Conference is one of the most famous in Canadian history. Look at it carefully. What does it reveal about the characters and backgrounds of the people who started the process of nation building? Who is included? Who appears to be left out? What evidence is there that John A. Macdonald played a central role?

SOCIAL EVENTS

Even more important than the daytime meetings were the nightly parties. In a land where travelling from one colony to another could take weeks, the men did not know each other well. Social events helped build a feeling of trust between them. Every night, the delegates mingled at parties, banquets, and concerts. The final ball ended at three in the morning after an evening of dining, dancing, speeches, and champagne. One observer noted that the delegates were "as befogged as the harbour."

CONFEDERATION ON TOUR

Before their meeting in Quebec City, the leaders went on the road to sell the idea of Confederation in Halifax, Fredericton, and Saint John. The Confederation scheme was rapidly gaining approval. Even distant Newfoundland, which had not sent delegates to the Charlottetown Conference, decided to send observers to the next round of meetings in Quebec.

1. How was nation building in Canada different from nation building in the United States? Which approach do you prefer? Why?

2. Describe the key results of the Charlottetown Conference.

3. In your opinion, is it a good idea to mix politics with parties as the delegates did at Charlottetown? Why or why not?

In Quebec City, the delegates discussed and debated all day and long into the night, stopping only to rest on Sunday. Occasionally, even such a leading figure as John A. Macdonald wandered off into a daydream. This draft of the 72 resolutions that were passed at the Quebec Conference shows the little drawings Macdonald doodled in the margins as he listened to the debates. Does this knowledge change your view of Macdonald? Explain.

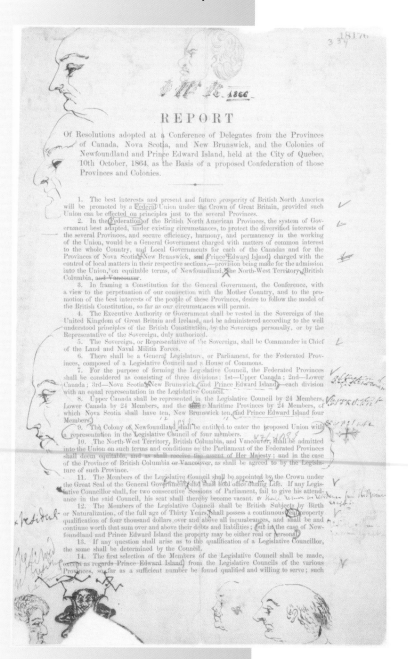

QUEBEC: THE SECOND STEP

October 10–24, 1864

With great optimism, the delegates gathered in Quebec City. The autumn weather was cold and gloomy, a change from the warm, pleasant days they had enjoyed in Charlottetown. The easy times were behind them as the delegates sat down to work out the details of Confederation. The closer they got to drafting the final terms, the more problems they saw. In a letter to his wife, George Brown wrote:

> "*It will be a tremendous thing if we can accomplish it. I don't believe any of us appreciate the immensity of the work we are engaged in.*"

The Problems

Not all the colonies were ready to give up their independence to a central government that might be controlled by Canada West, which had the largest population. The smaller the colony, the greater its fear of being swallowed by the new union.

Canada West argued for representation by population, so that the provinces with the most people would have the most representatives in government. The less-populated colonies wanted all the new provinces to have equal representation in a Senate.

All the colonies were asking for the central government to take over their debts for railway and road construction. Prince Edward Islanders were looking for a promise that they would be able to buy the farmland that was owned by British landlords.

The Resolutions

The days and nights of hard bargaining at the Quebec Conference resulted in a proposal to unite the colonies of British North America. The new central government would be a **constitutional monarchy**, with the British king or queen acting as the country's official head of state. The proposal included 72 resolutions. Here are the key elements:

Division of Power

The central government would take over most of the powers that had been held by Britain and all areas that affected the new nation as a whole, such as defence, the postal service, and trade with other countries. The new provincial governments would hold on to colonial powers, such as education, business, and roads.

Representation

Members of the House of Commons would be elected by male voters on the basis of representation by population. Women, Aboriginal people, and people who did not own land could not vote.

The Senate

Canada West and Canada East would have 24 senators each, and 24 more senators would represent the interests of the two Atlantic provinces. Senators would be appointed rather than elected. No law could be passed without Senate approval.

Money Matters

The central government would take over the debts of the provinces. The provinces would lose the right to raise money by collecting tariffs.

Railways

The government would build railways to link the new provinces.

BALLS AND BANQUETS

Delegates caught up in the whirl of making history during the day looked forward to socializing together in the evenings. The delegates from Canada East and West were especially charming and entertaining. They chatted with the delegates' wives. George-Étienne Cartier played the piano, sang, and danced. John A. Macdonald and Thomas D'Arcy McGee told stories.

"The Cabinet Ministers, the leading ones especially, … do not seem to miss a dance during the live-long night," wrote Edward Whelan, a P.E.I. delegate. "They are cunning fellows and … know that if they can dance themselves into the affections of the wives and daughters of the country, the men will certainly be an easy conquest."

Not everyone enjoyed the festivities. The daughter of the British governor described the not-so-charming behaviour of John A. Macdonald: "He is always drunk now, I am sorry to say, and when someone went to his room the other night, they found him in his nightshirt with a railway rug thrown over him, practising Hamlet before a looking glass." Later, she added: "I shall not cry when these delegates are gone—it is a bore having to dance with them."

Many delegates brought their wives and children to the Confederation conferences. Everyone looked forward to social events in the evenings, especially the lavish banquets and balls.

CONFEDERATION ON TOUR (AGAIN)

When the Quebec discussions wrapped up, delegates went on the road again. This time they toured Canada East and West, stopping to meet the influential men of Montreal, Ottawa, Prescott, Kingston, Belleville, Cobourg, Toronto, Hamilton, and Niagara Falls.

The delegates were proud of the resolutions they had negotiated in Quebec City. When their tour ended, they returned to their colonies to sell the idea of Confederation to the people.

The touring delegates visited Ottawa, the site of the proposed new capital, and toured the magnificent new Parliament buildings then under construction. Once planned as the capital of the United Province of Canada, Ottawa would now be the capital of a new nation.

Delegates to the Quebec Conference

Canada West	George Brown	Sir John A. Macdonald
	Sir Alexander Campbell	William McDougall
	James Cockburn	Sir Oliver Mowat
	Sir William Howland	
Canada East	Sir George-Étienne Cartier	Sir Hector Langevin
	Jean Charles Chapais	Thomas D'Arcy McGee
	Sir Alexander Galt	Sir Étienne Tache
New Brunswick	Edward Chandler	Peter Mitchell
	John Hamilton Gray	William Henry Steeves
	John Mercer Johnson	Sir Leonard Tilley
Newfoundland	Sir Frederick Carter	Sir Ambrose Shea
Nova Scotia	Sir Adams Archibald	Jonathan McCully
	Robert Barry Dickey	Sir Charles Tupper
	W.A. Henry	
Prince Edward Island	John Hamilton Gray	Edward Palmer
	Thomas Haviland	William Henry Pope
	A.A. Macdonald	Edward Whelan

The deal makers at the Quebec meeting were not typical of the average inhabitant of British North America. For instance, there were no women, no visible minorities, no Aboriginal people, no poor, and no handicapped people. Most representatives were professionals—lawyers, merchants, doctors, and journalists—and some were wealthy.

The Deal Makers

Canada West
Sir John A. Macdonald

Sir John A. Macdonald
Born: Scotland, 1815
Died: Canada, 1891

Background:

Born in Scotland, John A. Macdonald came to Canada when he was five years old. A bright student, he began articling in a legal firm when he was 15 and managed a law office at 17. He was a lawyer by the age of 21. He had fought against the rebels in 1837 and entered the legislature of the Province of Canada in 1844.

Role in Confederation:

Macdonald was a clever and persuasive politician. He and George-Étienne Cartier, from Canada East, formed a powerful alliance that dominated the politics of Canada. With the united Parliament of Canada increasingly paralyzed, the two men entered into the Great Coalition with George Brown to investigate Confederation.

Macdonald soon became the leading force in the Confederation process. He played a central role in all of the conferences. He helped draft most of the terms of Confederation and worked hard to keep French Canada and the Maritimes on board. Without his efforts, the Confederation dream might never have happened.

Role after Confederation:

Macdonald served as Canada's first prime minister and oversaw the early development of the new nation from 1867 to 1872 and from 1878 until his death in 1891. He supervised Canada's expansion from sea to sea and encouraged the building of a transcontinental railway. His two battles with Louis Riel, during the rebellions in the west in 1869 and 1885, divided public opinion. Macdonald worked hard to maintain the English-French partnership that was at the heart of Confederation. His program of protective tariffs, railroads, and incentives to bring immigrants into the new western territories spurred the economic development of the nation. When he died in 1891, a grateful nation mourned the most important of the Fathers of Confederation.

Canada East
Sir George-Étienne Cartier

Sir George-Étienne Cartier
Born: Canada, 1814
Died: England, 1873

Background:

Born into a wealthy Montreal family, Cartier claimed to be a descendant of Jacques Cartier, the famous explorer. George-Étienne Cartier was a well-educated lawyer. Proudly French Canadian, he participated in the rebellion of 1837 in Lower Canada. Renouncing violence, he returned to Montreal to build a successful law practice, often working with railway companies. He entered the legislature of the Province of Canada in 1848 where he soon became a leading force. Cartier led a group of members from Canada East who worked with John A. Macdonald from Canada West. This union became the basis of the Conservative Party of Canada. Cartier was a fierce opponent of George Brown, who worked tirelessly to reduce the influence of Canada East in the affairs of Canada West. Later, Cartier joined Brown and Macdonald in the Great Coalition to end the political deadlock in the Canadas.

Role in Confederation:

Cartier attended all three Confederation conferences. Without Cartier's active support, it is doubtful that Confederation could have been achieved. He was particularly important in persuading French Canada to accept the new political union because he worked to protect the special nature of Canada East. His connections with railway promoters added political muscle and money to the efforts of the pro-Confederation supporters. He was a passionate spokesperson for the concept of Confederation.

Role after Confederation:

As Canada's first minister of Militia and Defence, he played a role in the **Red River Rebellion** in 1869. He helped ensure the entry of Manitoba and British Columbia into Confederation. He was defeated in 1872. Cartier died before the **Pacific Scandal** broke and revealed how he and Macdonald had received money from railway promoters for an election campaign.

New Brunswick
Sir Leonard Tilley

Sir Leonard Tilley
Born: Gagetown, N.B., 1818
Died: Saint John, 1896

Background:

Tilley worked in a drug store at 13 and later became successful in a medical supply business. He entered the legislature of New Brunswick in 1850 and led the government from 1861 to 1865. He was a great supporter of railways, education, **temperance**, and Confederation. He lost an 1865 election to anti-Confederation forces, but Fenian raids, money from Canada, and support from Britain resulted in an election victory in 1866.

Role in Confederation:

Tilley was an active participant in the debates at Charlottetown and Quebec. He fought desperately—and successfully—against anti-Confederation forces in his own province of New Brunswick. Tilley is also credited with suggesting the name for the new nation, Dominion of Canada.

Role after Confederation:

Tilley served as minister of Customs in Macdonald's first Cabinet (1867–1872) and later as minister of Finance (1879–1885). He was appointed lieutenant governor of New Brunswick from 1873 to 1878 and from 1885 to 1883. Tilley was knighted in 1879.

Nova Scotia
Sir Charles Tupper

Sir Charles Tupper
Born: Nova Scotia, 1821
Died: England, 1915

Background:

Descended from a line of early Nova Scotians, Tupper was trained in medicine in Edinburgh, Scotland, and set up a successful medical practice in Amherst, Nova Scotia. He was the first president of the Canadian Medical Association (1867–1870). He entered politics in 1855 and became premier in 1864. He first promoted a larger union for the Maritimes and then promoted Confederation itself.

Role in Confederation:

Tupper was present at all three Confederation conferences. As well as playing an important political role, he kept his medical bag with him at all times and tended to the needs of the delegates and their families. He fought hard for Confederation against increasing suspicion and opposition in his home province. When it appeared Nova Scotia might refuse Confederation, he decided against bringing it to a vote in the legislature.

Role after Confederation:

In the first federal election after Confederation, 19 members from Nova Scotia were elected to the House of Commons. Only Tupper had been a supporter of Confederation. He worked behind the scenes to get a better deal for Nova Scotia and later served in a range of positions in Sir John A. Macdonald's Cabinet, including minister of Internal Revenue, Customs, Public Works, Railways and Canals, and Finance. In 1896, he became prime minister of Canada but held power for the shortest term in Canadian history—a mere 10 weeks. He died in England in 1915, the last of the original Fathers of Confederation.

Prince Edward Island
Edward Whelan

EDWARD WHELAN
A FATHER OF CONFEDERATION
JOURNALIST, ORATOR, AND ADVOCATE OF
FREE LAND, FREE SCHOOLS AND
RESPONSIBLE GOVERNMENT
BORN IN COUNTY MAYO, IRELAND, 1824.
DIED IN CHARLOTTETOWN, 10TH DEC., 1867

HISTORIC SITES AND MONUMENTS BOARD OF CANADA

Edward Whelan
Born: Ireland, 1824
Died: Charlottetown, P.E.I., 1867

Background:

Unlike most Fathers of Confederation, Whelan was a man of modest means. Whelan immigrated to Nova Scotia in 1831, and in 1832, he worked as a printing apprentice for the famous Joseph Howe. Largely self-educated, Whelan moved to Charlottetown in 1843 and started a publishing career. He was one of three publisher-politicians, along with Joseph Howe and George Brown, who involved themselves with the Confederation issue in the press and in political spheres. He entered P.E.I. politics in 1846, where he fought for **responsible government** and lobbied against absentee landlords who owned much of P.E.I.

Role in Confederation:

Whelan was a delegate to the Quebec Conference and eagerly supported Confederation. Much of the human side of the story was retold in his newspaper. Readers eagerly read his witty accounts of the parties and banquets. Even when P.E.I. delegates began to reject Confederation, Whelan still promoted the idea.

Role after Confederation:

Although P.E.I. rejected Confederation, Whelan continued to argue for the idea. He was defeated in the election of 1867 and died later that year in Charlottetown, birthplace of the Confederation dream. Sadly, Whelan was long gone when P.E.I. finally entered into union with Canada in 1873. Rumoured plans for an insider's account of the Confederation debates died with him.

1. **Why was the Quebec Conference such an important event?**

2. **Which terms of the Quebec agreement do you most support? Why?**

3. **Which terms do you least support? Why?**

4. **Would you like to have been one of the Fathers of Confederation? Explain.**

5. **Which of the Fathers of Confederation do you most admire? Why?**

6. **Who is a living Canadian you admire? Why?**

The Back Story

When the delegates arrived in Quebec City in the fall of 1864, one of the first things they did was have their photos taken for a set of "calling cards." These cards were a way of introducing themselves during the formal and informal sessions of the Quebec Conference. Many of the guests were keen to collect a full set of cards from what was clearly becoming an historic occasion: creating a blueprint for a new country.

The Goal

Choose a Father of Confederation. Make a calling card to introduce yourself to other delegates at the Quebec Conference.

The Steps

1. Choose a Father of Confederation to role-play.
2. Research your choice. Include your name, date, and place of birth; the colony you represent; a brief biography of your background and experience; and a statement of your major concerns and thoughts about the union of British North America. Include any other details that you think would add interest to your calling card.
3. Create an illustration for your card.
4. Organize your information and illustration to ensure your card is attractive and informative.

Evaluating Your Work

As you work, keep these criteria in mind. Be sure to:
- carefully review the instructions before starting your work
- complete your research and make careful notes
- show a solid understanding of the subject of your role-play
- design your card neatly and creatively. Remember to do a rough draft first and ask for reactions and suggestions from peers and your teacher.

History in Action

Confederation Calling Cards

CANADA EAST

THOMAS D'ARCY M[...]

CANADA EAST

[...]TIENNE CARTIER

CANADA WEST

NEW BRUNSWICK

LEONARD TILLE[...]

JOHN A. MACDONALD

I was born in Scotland, and came to Canada when I was five years old. I was a bright student, and began articling in a legal firm when I was 15 and managed a law office at 17. I became a lawyer at the age of 21. I fought against the rebels in 1837 and entered the legislature of the Province of Canada in 1844.

I REPRESENT CANADA WEST

NOVA SCOTIA

CHARLES TUPPER

CHAPTER 4

FINAL BATTLES FOR CONFEDERATION

S ome delegates who had attended the Quebec Conference in October 1864 were sure that Confederation could be achieved within the year. However, opposition was growing in the five colonies. Each colony had its reasons for supporting—and not supporting—the deal. The battles for Confederation were not over yet.

Many Newfoundlanders campaigned fiercely against Confederation in the 1860s and again in 1949. The colony finally joined Canada in 1949.

THE ROCK SAYS NO!

Newfoundland had sent no delegates to Charlottetown, but two delegates, Frederick Carter and Ambrose Shea, attended the meetings in Quebec, where the 72 resolutions had been negotiated. It would not be easy, however, to convince Newfoundland to join a union. Newfoundlanders didn't want to lose their independence. They worried about competing with Canadian businesses and feared that one day they would be forced to send their young men into an army to protect Canada from American raiders. In songs and petitions, the people voiced their opposition. Newfoundland stayed independent until 1949, when it finally entered Confederation under the newest "Father of Confederation," Premier Joey Smallwood.

PRINCE EDWARD ISLAND

The delegates from Prince Edward Island left the Quebec Conference disappointed. They felt the resolutions did not meet their needs, especially their desire for money to buy out the absentee landlords so their land could be turned over to Islanders. They also realized that the tiny colony would have almost no power in this new nation, with just 5 of 194 seats in the House of Commons and 4 of 72 seats in the Senate. An intercolonial railway wouldn't do an island much good either. The P.E.I. legislature refused to even discuss a deal that gave them so little. It took six more years and a new agreement before Prince Edward Island entered Confederation in 1873.

P.E.I. celebrated its independence from Confederation in 1867. Six years later, the colony became a new province in Canada.

FROM THE SOURCES: THE PEOPLE SPEAK

As you read the song and petition from anti-Confederation forces in Newfoundland, note the main reasons for rejecting the union. In your opinion, which of these arguments are valid? Which are invalid? Explain.

Anti-Confederation Song

Hurrah for our own native isle, Newfoundland!
Not a stranger shall hold one inch of its strand!
Her face turns to Britain, her back to the Gulf,
Come near at your peril, Canadian Wolf!

Ye brave Newfoundlanders who plough the salt sea
With hearts like the eagle so bold and so free,
The time is at hand when you'll all have to say
If Confederation will carry the day.

Cheap tea and molasses they say they will give,
All taxes take off that the poor man shall live;
Cheap nails and cheap lumber our coffins to make,
And homespun to mend our old clothes when they break.

If they take off the taxes how then will they meet
The heavy expense of the country's upkeep?
Just give them the chance to get us in the scrape
And they'll chain us like slaves with pen, ink, and red tape.

Would you barter your rights that your fathers have won,
Your freedom transmitted from father to son?
For a few thousand dollars of Canadian gold,
Don't let it be said that your birthright was sold.

Then hurrah for our own native isle, Newfoundland,
Not a stranger shall hold one inch of its strand!
Her face turns to Britain, her back to the Gulf,
Come near at your peril, Canadian Wolf!

TO THE PARLIAMENT OF GREAT BRITAIN

THIS PETITION of the undersigned merchants, traders, fishermen and other inhabitants of Newfoundland

MOST HUMBLY STATES

That this colony has for many years enjoyed the blessings and privileges of self-government and local legislation. It has generally managed its own affairs.

That the feelings of its people have been, and still are, most loyal and devoted. Its needs and demands for protection from foreign enemies or internal problems have never placed a heavy burden or cost on the British Empire. It has never had any political ties, only minor commercial links, with Canada. Its connection with Canada is cut off by sea for nearly six months of the year. The inhabitants of this colony wish to see the island always kept separately by Britain as its ocean fortress and military outpost in this part of the world, no matter what may become of the colonies on the mainland.

NEW BRUNSWICK

Leonard Tilley returned to New Brunswick from the Quebec Conference ready to sell the idea of Confederation, but found himself facing a storm of protest. The enemies of Confederation, many of them merchants, were afraid that the large and powerful Province of Canada would easily dominate the new nation and put them out of business. Tilley called a sudden election, hoping the anti-Confederation group would have no time to organize a fight. It turned out to be a terrible mistake. Confusion, fear, and misinformation convinced voters that Confederation would be a disaster for the colony. When the votes were counted, only 11 of the 41 elected representatives were pro-Confederation. Tilley lost his own seat. Confederation was dead in New Brunswick—for now.

NOVA SCOTIA

Premier Charles Tupper in Nova Scotia also faced a hail of protest. Nova Scotians were afraid of handing control over to a new government that would probably be dominated by Canada East and West. The secrecy of the Quebec Conference also bothered them. All the negotiations had taken place behind closed doors. Both the public and the press had been excluded, which led some people to suspect that Confederation was a plot that had been dreamed up by the railway promoters hoping to win government money.

Tupper had a tough opponent in Joseph Howe, an experienced politician and publisher. In his newspaper, the *Halifax Morning Chronicle*, he mocked the proposal as "Botheration" rather than "Confederation." Tupper decided against putting the 72 resolutions before the government for a vote. He waited, while the anti-Confederation storm raged about him.

Joseph Howe

"We are sold for the price of a sheepskin."

Antoine-Aimé Dorion was a French-Canadian opponent of Confederation. When Tilley lost the election in New Brunswick, he gleefully declared,

"*I say that this scheme is killed. I repeat that it is killed.*"

PROVINCE OF CANADA

Even in Canada East and West, where the idea of Confederation had started, there was anger, debate, and many questions. Critics in Canada East wondered if their culture and language would survive in a union with so many English-speaking provinces. Many Canadians questioned the plan to build an intercolonial railway: Could the new nation afford to build a railway line from Canada West to Nova Scotia without heavily taxing the citizens?

Confederation proposed **free trade** among the provinces. That meant the end of the tariffs that each colony collected on goods imported from other colonies. Tariffs protected local industries and were a major source of money for the colonial governments. How would the Province of Canada make up the money it lost in tariffs?

This cartoon illustrates French-Canadian opposition to Confederation. Why are cartoons a good way to promote a political message?

Telling Their Stories

SIR WILFRID LAURIER

Watch *Canada: A People's History*, Episode 8: The Great Enterprise, "Let Their Memory Be Dark" (1:17:18 to 1:23:41) to hear the voices of French Canadians who opposed Confederation. What were their reasons? Do you think their reasons were justified?

VOICES FOR CONFEDERATION

The pro-Confederation forces dangled the dream of a powerful new nation before the members of the Legislative Assembly. George-Étienne Cartier and his allies worked hard to convince French Canadians that Confederation was the best way to protect their language and culture. They would share power in a central government, he argued, and they would manage education, religion, and language within their own province.

D'Arcy McGee spoke eloquently about a new nationality: " A Canadian nationality—not French Canadian nor Irish Canadian—is in my opinion what we should look forward to, that is what we ought to be prepared to defend to the death."

The tireless Macdonald spoke convincingly about how Confederation would solve the problems of the scattered colonies: "The Confederation of all the British North American Provinces … has been looked upon by many far-seeing politicians as being eventually the means of deciding and settling very many of the vexed questions."

For days, the government members argued the pros and cons of Confederation. When the debate ended on March 10, 1865, Confederation had passed by a vote of 91 to 33, which included a majority of the French-Canadian politicians.

It was a clear victory for Confederation. Or was it? Only Canada was in favour. Newfoundland, Prince Edward Island, and New Brunswick were out. Tupper in Nova Scotia was trying to avoid a vote on the issue. What forces would finally move Confederation forward?

◄ Playback ►

1. **Explain the reaction to the Confederation plan in Newfoundland, Prince Edward Island, New Brunswick, Nova Scotia, and Canada.**

2. **What could the Fathers of Confederation have done differently at the Quebec Conference to get more positive results? Explain.**

3. **In your view, was there any real alternative to Confederation at this time? Explain.**

UNDER ATTACK!

In the middle of the political battle to win Confederation, a real battle suddenly exploded on the Canadian frontier. Early in June 1866, hundreds of heavily armed and battle-hardened Irish Americans marched across the Niagara River, seized Fort Erie, and cut off telegraph and railway lines. Swiftly, they marched on to the town of Ridgeway, where they easily defeated an inexperienced force of Canadian soldiers. They killed 9 and wounded 38.

The invaders were Fenians, Irish Americans who thought that by attacking the colonies they could force the hated British out of their native Ireland. Fenians had launched attacks on New Brunswick a few months earlier. Another force was poised to strike Quebec. Most had gained military experience fighting for the northern states in the American Civil War.

Their success was quickly cut short when a force of 20 000 Canadian militiamen and British regulars headed towards the border. The Fenian leaders hurried back to the United States and were placed under temporary arrest by American authorities. Still recovering from the blood-shed of the Civil War, the Americans had no desire to get into a war with Britain.

Fenian raids posed a real threat to the colonies in British North America. The politicians realized that they could best protect themselves through a confederation in which the united colonies would stand together against foreign invaders.

From the Sources
SONGS OF WAR

The Fenians and Canadians both marched to war tunes when they went to war in 1866. Read these lyrics and note the similarities and differences. Why do you suppose music is often used during war?

Fenian Marching Song

We are the Fenian Brotherhood,
*   skilled in the arts of war,*
And we're going to fight for Ireland,
*   that land that we adore.*
Many battles we have won,
*   along with the boys in blue,*
And we'll go and capture Canada for
*   we've nothing else to do.*

Canadian Marching Song

Tramp, tramp, tramp,
Our boys are marching,
Cheer up, let the Fenians come!
For beneath the Union Jack,
We'll drive the rabble back,
And we'll fight for our
*   beloved Canadian home.*

The Fenian raids frightened the colonies. Fear of an American invasion became a strong argument for Confederation.

> **LITTLE BOY:** "Father, what country do we live in?"
> **FATHER:** "My dear son, you have no country, for Mr. Tilley has sold all to the Canadians for eighty cents a head."
>
> *This story, told by Andrew R. Wetmore during the New Brunswick election in 1865, reflected popular feeling against Confederation.*

TILLEY WINS IN NEW BRUNSWICK

The Fenian raids helped Leonard Tilley and his pro-Confederation cause in New Brunswick. Union would bring military protection against outside threats. British representatives in the colony were urging New Brunswick to join Confederation, and anti-Confederation politicians were having trouble governing because they didn't agree on anything other than their opposition to Confederation. In a fierce election campaign held in 1866, Tilley—fortified with money from Canada's railway men—swept back into power. The anti-Confederation politicians won only 8 of 41 seats.

Sir Charles Tupper

TUPPER MOVES IN NOVA SCOTIA

With Confederation won in the Canadas and New Brunswick, and the other colonies worried about looming Fenian attacks, Sir Charles Tupper decided to act. He sent a delegation to London, England, to take part in another Confederation conference. The anti-Confederation forces from Nova Scotia also sent a delegation.

THE LONDON CONFERENCE, 1866

The pro-Confederation delegates from the Province of Canada, New Brunswick, and Nova Scotia arrived in London, England determined to turn the Quebec resolutions into a constitution for a new nation. Members of the British Parliament, anxious to see the colonies unite and look after themselves, were happy to assist. Despite protests from the Nova Scotia team, the process ran smoothly and quickly under the leadership of John A. Macdonald.

By February 1867, most issues were resolved. The British North America Act was introduced into the British Parliament on February 12 and given royal assent on March 29, 1867. July 1 was chosen for the official proclamation of the Dominion of Canada. It was also the day that Macdonald was knighted and added the title "Sir" to his name.

Sixteen delegates met in London, England in December 1866 and turned the Quebec resolutions into the British North America Act. Passed by Britain's Parliament, it created the new Dominion of Canada.

What's in a Name?

What would the new nation be called? Many names were suggested, including Northland, Anglia, Tuponia, Albinora, Mesopelagia, British Efsiga, and Cabotia! Thankfully, none of these names caught on. Most people wanted to call the new country the "Kingdom of Canada," but the British worried that "Kingdom" would offend the Americans. Tilley suggested "Dominion of Canada." It remains the official name of Canada today.

Sir John: The Personal Side

In the midst of all the debates and resolutions, it is easy to forget the human side of the people who made Confederation a reality. For example, Sir John A. Macdonald is remembered for his political skill, but he was also a husband, a father, and a man of charm and wit with his share of personal troubles.

Macdonald's first wife, Isabella, became an invalid shortly after their marriage. Isabella died in 1857. Their son died at 13 months. While in London, Macdonald met a former aquaintance, Agnes Bernard. They married in 1867. Tragedy stuck again when Agnes gave birth to a daughter, Mary, who had severe physical and mental disabilities. The tough, seasoned politician doted on his daughter. She missed him terribly when he travelled and told him so in letters she wrote with the help of a nurse.

Macdonald went on to become Canada's first—and, to many, its greatest—prime minister. After a long career in office, he died in 1891 and a nation mourned.

THE MOTHERS OF CONFEDERATION

Hortense Cartier

Anne Nelson Brown

Rosemarie Kuptana

Little has been written about the women who played a role in Canada's nation building. When Confederation was being debated, women had few political rights and could neither vote nor hold office, but they still wielded influence.

Agnes Macdonald, Hortense Cartier, Jane Mowat, Alice Tilley, Frances Tupper, Mary McGee, Anne Nelson Brown, and Catherine Howe have been called the Mothers of Confederation. They advised their husbands during the Confederation debates. At the banquets and balls while they dined and danced, they were helping build social relationships among the delegates, as well as a sense of trust that was so important to the progress of the union. Some historians believe that Anne Nelson Brown changed George Brown from an argumentative politician into the reasonable negotiator who was able to create the Great Coalition.

More than 100 years later, during the **Meech Lake Accord** and **Charlottetown Accord** talks, modern Canadian women, such as Aboriginal leader Rosemarie Kuptana, played a more central role. Any future changes to Confederation will involve the full participation of Canadian women.

◀ Playback ▶

1. **How did the Fenian raids affect the move to unite the colonies?**
2. **Briefly describe the results of the London Conference.**
3. **Suggest an alternative name for Canada. Explain your choice.**
4. **Would you like to become a Canadian politician? Explain.**

The First Canada Day, July 1, 1867

In cities and towns across the new nation, Canadians celebrated their first birthday with speeches, banquets, picnics, parades, and fireworks.

One young girl recalled the special day: "'This is the First of July, in the year eighteen hundred and sixty seven,' father said. 'Always remember this day and this night. You are a very lucky little girl, to be a child in Canada today.'"

On July 1, 1867, crowds gathered in the towns and cities of New Brunswick, Nova Scotia, Canada East, and Canada West to celebrate the birth of their new nation.

THE FREE PRESS

The birth of Canada was front-page news in every corner of the new country. In their pages, the newspapers expressed different points of view. What are the major differences in these reports of Canada's first birthday?

HALIFAX MORNING CHRONICLE

~ July 1, 1867 ~

DIED. Last night at twelve o'clock the free and enlightened province of Nova Scotia. Deceased was the offspring of old English stock and promised to have proved an honour and support to her parents in their declining years. Her death was occasioned by unnatural treatment received at the hands of some of her ungrateful sons, who, taking advantage of the position she had afforded them, betrayed her to the enemy. Funeral will take place from the Grand Parade this day, Monday at 9 o'clock. Friends are requested not to attend, as her enemies, with becoming scorn, intend to insult the occasion with rejoicing.

Le Journal Des
TROIS-RIVIÈRES
—— JULY 1, 1867 ——

WE SHALL LIKE TO REMEMBER, when Confederation has stood the test of time, how beautiful was the day when it began.

TORONTO
The Globe
~ July 1, 1867 ~

WE HAIL THE BIRTHDAY OF A NEW NATIONALITY!

– by George Brown

LIFE GOES ON

As important as Confederation was, many people were more engrossed in other matters than in the politics of the day. The year 1867 was remarkable, and not just because of Confederation.

In 1867, Emily Stowe became the first female doctor to open a medical practice in Canada. Because Canadian medical schools did not admit women, she had been forced to get her training in the United States. Later, Emily Stowe became a leader in the movement to win voting rights for Canadian women.

The Saint John Four, a New Brunswick rowing crew, exploded onto the international rowing scene in 1867 with a stunning victory at the World Amateur Rowing Championships in Paris. The young nation was ecstatic about the "pride of Saint John."

The National Lacrosse Association was established in 1867. Lacrosse remains popular today and is, in fact, Canada's national sport.

In 1867, the United States purchased Alaska from Russia for $7.2 million, alarming Canadians who feared the U.S. was gobbling up much of North America. A number of Alaskan settlers moved to Canada.

Emily Stowe

Father of Confederation Assassinated

On April 7, 1868, less than a year after Canada's first birthday, one of the new nation's most passionate and poetic supporters was the victim of Canada's first political assassination. Thomas D'Arcy McGee was shot in Ottawa as he headed home from a late-night session of Parliament.

Patrick Whelan, a Fenian, was tried, convicted, and hanged for his murder. On the scaffold, his last words were "God Bless Ireland and God save my soul." It was the last public hanging in Canadian history. Today, some people question whether Whelan was actually guilty. There would not be another political assassination in Canada until the murder of Pierre Laporte by the **FLQ** in 1970.

Borrowed from Native people, lacrosse was a major sport in 1867.

The Back Story

In the 1860s, most Canadians were not directly consulted about Confederation, and few were able to express an opinion publicly. Today, citizens can write to newspapers to state their views on important issues. The best letters are often published on a letters-to-the-editor page or on the newspaper's web site. Sometimes, radio and television reporters stand on a busy street and interview people about their views on current issues. These news reports are called "streeters."

The Goal

You will write a letter to the editor or record an audio or video news report that expresses your views about the battles surrounding Confederation. You may role-play a figure from the days of Confederation or take the role of a contemporary Canadian.

The Steps

1. Identify your role. Who are you? Where are you from? What is your job? You could be a contemporary Canadian student, a fisher from Newfoundland, a logger from New Brunswick, or a farmer from Canada West, etc.
2. Research and prepare a statement of your attitude about Confederation. Do you support it or reject it? Why? Support your position with at least two well-organized arguments. Finish your statement with a powerful conclusion.
3. Write a letter to the editor (at least one page long) or write the comments you plan to record as an audio or video news report. Rehearse the news report so that your presentation is smooth.
4. Share your letter to the editor or your "streeter" with a small group, a partner, or the class. Be prepared to support your opinion in an information debate with your classmates.

Evaluating Your Work

As you work, keep these criteria in mind. Be sure to:
- review and follow the steps carefully
- research and create a personal background for your character
- complete and review at least two drafts of your letter
- practise your "streeter" before recording it.

History in Action

Your Opinion on Confederation

HALIFAX MORNING CHRONICLE
~ July 1, 1867 ~

DIED. Last night at twelve o'clock the free and enlightened province of Nova Scotia. Deceased was the offspring of old English stock and promised to have proved an honour and support to her parents in their declining years. Her death was occasioned by unnatural treatment received at the hands of some of her ungrateful sons, who, taking advantage of the position she had afforded them, betrayed her to the enemy. Funeral will take place from the Grand Parade this day, Monday at 9 o'clock. Friends are requested not to attend, as her ... with becoming scorn,

TORONTO The Globe
~ July 1, 1867 ~

WE HAIL THE BIRTHDAY OF A NEW NATIONALITY!

– by George Brown

Le Journal Des TROIS-RIVIÈRES
— JULY 1, 1867 —

WE SHALL LIKE TO REMEMBER, when Confederation has stood the test of time, how beautiful was the day when it began.

CHAPTER 5

Fast Forward

The British North America Act that created Canada in 1867 was just the beginning for the new Dominion. In 1870, Manitoba joined Confederation. British Columbia joined in 1871. Alberta and Saskatchewan followed in 1905. And the Rock finally said yes in 1949. Today, the story of Confederation continues to unfold as Canadians face new and old challenges in nation building.

Confederation in 1867 was just the beginning of nation building for Canada. Since then, it has added six more provinces, boundaries have changed, and new territories have been created.

TIMELINE

1870 Manitoba joins Confederation

1873 P.E.I. joins Confederation

1885 Canadian Pacific Railway completed

1905 Alberta and Saskatchewan join Confederation

1949 Newfoundland and Labrador join Confederation

1869 Canada buys Rupert's Land from the Hudson's Bay Company

1871 British Columbia joins Confederation

1875 New boundaries for NWT

1898 Yukon created as a new territory

1918 Women win the right to vote in federal elections

The Last Father of Confederation

JOEY SMALLWOOD

In 1949, when Newfoundland joined Confederation, Joey Smallwood became the first premier of the new province. He had spent years campaigning for union with Canada, trying to convince his fellow Newfoundlanders that it was a better option than remaining a poor colony of Britain. As premier for the next 22 years, Smallwood liked to boast that he was the only "living Father of Confederation." He died in 1991.

THE SONS AND DAUGHTERS OF CONFEDERATION

Today, Canada is a country that the Fathers of Confederation could not have imagined in 1867. For over 140 years, the process of nation building has been in the hands of all the sons and daughters of Confederation. They have built a country that is prosperous and peaceful and home to people from around the world. As they were helping shape the country, these generations of Canadians were also wrestling with problems in the ongoing story of Confederation.

The future of Confederation and Canadian nation building are now in the hands of a new generation.

TIMELINE

1967 Canada celebrates its 100th birthday

1970 FLQ terrorists kidnap two men in Quebec (the October Crisis)

1980 Quebec votes no in a referendum on separation

"O Canada" becomes the official national anthem

1990 Meech Lake Accord fails

1995 Separatism referendum narrowly defeated in Quebec

1965 New Canadian flag adopted

1969 Parliament passes the Official Languages Act

1974 Parliament passes the Multiculturalism Act

1982 Constitution comes home to Canada and Charter of Rights and Freedoms becomes law

1992 Charlottetown Accord rejected in national referendum

1999 Territory of Nunavut created

As the sons and daughters of Confederation, what are our responsibilities and rights? How do we respond to the continuing problems facing Confederation? Do we leave it to our leaders, as most people did in 1867, or do we want to be involved and consulted? Do we owe Canada anything?

THE CONTINUING CHALLENGES OF CONFEDERATION

While the forces that drew Canadians together seem to belong to the past, some of the concerns that were important in 1867 are still issues today.

French-English Relations

The federal structure that the Fathers of Confederation worked out for Canada seemed to allow for unity and difference at the same time. Soon after Confederation, however, new tensions divided English and French Canadians.

The desire to separate from Canada has been a strong issue in Quebec for the last 50 years. Quebec has elected separatists to both its provincial government and the Parliament of Canada. In 1980 and 1995, the people of Quebec voted in a **referendum** that asked them whether or not the province should separate from Canada. Though the majority of French Canadians have chosen to stay within Confederation, national unity is a continuing concern.

In 1995, Quebeckers who wanted Quebec to separate from Canada voted "oui" in the referendum.

Canadian-American Relations

Fear of a military threat from the United States helped push the colonies to unite in 1867. Today, the American threat to Canada is cultural and economic, rather than military. We watch American television, buy American books, copy American fashions, and go to American movies. The United States has 10 times more people than Canada and far more economic and military strength. Some people are afraid that American dominance will mean the end of a unique Canadian identity. Canadian-American relations will always play a central role in the future of Canada.

Canadian and American flags flying side by side

A homeless man in Toronto

Economic Prosperity

Some of the strongest reasons for Confederation in 1867 were economic. Today, the United Nations has ranked Canada as one of the best places to live in the world. Though Confederation appears to have been a wonderful bargain, the riches of our nation have not been enjoyed by everyone. Some provinces have more wealth than others. In our largest cities, homeless people find shelter in the shadow of bank towers. Many First Nations people live in sub-standard conditions. Communities have suffered economic crises when mines and fishing grounds closed. Many Canadians are troubled by the gap between rich and poor.

Constitutional Change

For most of Canada's history, the only way to change the Constitution was to ask the British Parliament to amend the British North America Act of 1867. In 1982, most provinces and the federal government agreed to bring the Constitution home to Canada. In future, constitutional changes would be made by Canadians themselves. The Constitution Act of 1982 included a Charter of Rights and Freedoms, a list of guaranteed rights. Quebec disagreed with the constitutional changes, arguing that they did not apply to that province.

In 1987, Prime Minister Brian Mulroney and Quebec Premier Robert Bourassa tried to revive the spirit of French-English coopera-tion by returning to the constitutional bargaining table in a meeting at Meech Lake. The Meech Lake Accord gave Quebec special status based on its unique French heritage. The deal fell through when some provinces refused to accept special treatment for Quebec. The most dramatic moment came when Elijah Harper, a member of the Manitoba Legislature and an Aboriginal Canadian, refused to vote for the Accord. He carried an eagle feather to represent the power of the Aboriginal people.

In 1992, there was a second attempt to get Quebec to sign the Constitution Act. It produced the Charlottetown Accord, which also ended in failure. The constitutional issues have not disappeared. Perhaps another generation of Canadians will find solutions with the same success as the Fathers of Confederation.

Prime Minister Pierre Elliott Trudeau and Queen Elizabeth sign the Constitution Act of 1982

PROVIDENCE
BEING THEIR GUIDE
THEY BUILDED
BETTER THAN
THEY KNEW.

These words are engraved on a plaque that hangs in Prince Edward Island's Province House, where the Fathers of Confederation first met in 1864. The plaque was unveiled in 1927 to celebrate Canada's sixtieth birthday.

CANADA TODAY

July 1, 1867, began a history that the people of Canada continue to write every day. So much has changed since 1867. Today, there are 10 provinces and 3 territories. Today, women can vote and sit in Parliament. Today, the First Nations are a political force with concerns that cannot be ignored. Today, Canadians represent many religions, languages, and cultures.

This image of the opening of Canada's first Parliament in Ottawa suggests the bright future awaiting the new nation.

◄Playback►

1. **Compare the issues facing Canadians in 1867 with the issues facing Canadians today. Present your ideas using the following organizer. In your opinion, what is the greatest challenge? Explain fully.**

Challenge	1867	Today	My Thoughts and Solutions
French-English Relations			
Canadian-American Relations			
Economic Prosperity			
Political Deadlock			

2. **What are your most important rights and responsibilities as a son or daughter of Confederation?**

3. **How do you personally see the future of Canada? Write a one-page essay describing your view.**

The Back Story

A national anthem is an important symbol of a country's identity. In most countries, singing the anthem is an act of citizenship. Canada has only had its national anthem, "O Canada," since 1980. Before then, Canadians sang other national songs, including "God Save the Queen" (now called our "Royal Anthem") and "The Maple Leaf Forever," written in 1867.

Not everyone is happy with all the lyrics of "O Canada." Some Canadians object to the phrase "in all thy sons' command" because it leaves out women.

The Goal

Carefully analyse the lyrics of the two songs that have been sung as anthems in Canada, then suggest new lyrics for a national anthem that reflects Canada as you know it.

The Steps

1. Read the lyrics of each song and answer the following questions.
   a. What is your opinion of the lyrics? Explain.
   b. How suitable would each song have been as a national anthem in 1867? Explain.
   c. Would "The Maple Leaf Forever" be a suitable anthem today? Explain.
2. Review the lyrics of "O Canada." What changes do you think it needs? Why?
3. Change some of the lyrics of "O Canada" so that it better reflects your ideas about Canada. Or write a new anthem. Explain why your changes or new lyrics make a suitable symbol for Canada.

Evaluating Your Work

As you work, keep these criteria in mind. Be sure to:
- review the lyrics of "The Maple Leaf Forever" and "O Canada" before answering the questions
- respond fully and carefully to each of the questions, answering in complete sentences
- brainstorm what images and words best represent your Canada and create a list of possibilities before writing your lyrics
- complete at least two drafts of your lyrics
- try to make a unique contribution to the topic.

History in Action

Anthem for a Nation

The Maple Leaf Forever
In days of yore,
From Britain's shore
Wolfe the dauntless hero came
And planted firm Britannia's flag
On Canada's fair domain.
Here may it wave,
Our boast, our pride
And joined in love together,
The thistle, shamrock, rose entwined,
The Maple Leaf forever.

O Canada!
O Canada!
Our home and native land!
True patriot love in all thy sons' command
With glowing hearts we see thee rise,
The True North strong and free!
From far and wide,
O Canada, we stand on guard for thee.
God keep our land glorious and free!
O Canada, we stand on guard for thee.
O Canada, we stand on guard for thee.

Glossary

American Revolution The rebellion of the Thirteen Colonies against Great Britain in 1776, in which they declared their independence. The American War of Independence followed, from 1776 to 1783. At the end, the United States of America was an independent nation.

Charlottetown Accord The second failed attempt by Prime Minister Brian Mulroney and provincial premiers to reform the Canadian Constitution in 1992. Their proposals were defeated in a national referendum.

Confederate The name given to supporters of the South in the American Civil War. The Confederate side wanted the South to separate from the United States.

Confederation A type of political union in which separate communities join together. Usually, the central government is weak and the other levels are more powerful. In Canada, the reverse is true. We have a strong federal government, while the power of the provinces is weaker.

Constitutional Monarchy A government system that has a monarch as head of state and whose powers are limited by a written constitution.

FLQ The short form of Front de Libération du Québec. This was a small group of violent Quebec separatists who kidnapped British Trade Commissioner James Cross and assassinated Quebec Cabinet minister Pierre Laporte in October 1970. Cross was eventually released.

Free Trade Trade without tariffs between two countries.

Industrial Revolution The period in England from 1750 to 1850 that saw a change from a primarily agricultural economy to one based on manufacturing. It forced many people from the land to the cities or overseas to North America.

Manifest Destiny A belief, held by many Americans during the mid-1800s, that sooner or later the U.S. flag would fly all over North America.

Maritimers People who lived in the British colonies of P.E.I., Nova Scotia, and New Brunswick.

Meech Lake Accord A failed attempt by Prime Minister Brian Mulroney and many provincial premiers to reform the Canadian Constitution in 1987–1990.

Métis People descended from European and Aboriginal marriages.

Pacific Scandal Sir John A. Macdonald and other members of his Conservative Party were accused of taking money from railway promoters to finance their campaigns in the election of 1872. The scandal forced Macdonald to resign as prime minister in 1873.

Red River Rebellion A rebellion in 1869 against the Canadian government by Métis under the leadership of Louis Riel. It led to the entry of Manitoba as a new Canadian province.

Referendum A public vote on an issue, not an election.

Responsible Government A government that is accountable, or responsible, to elected representatives chosen by the people. This type of government was won in the United Province of Canada in 1849.

Rupert's Land The land given to the Hudson's Bay Company in 1670 by the British monarch, King Charles II. It included all the lands near the waters that emptied into Hudson Bay. It was named after Prince Rupert, the King's cousin and the first governor of the new company.

Tariffs Special taxes placed on goods coming into a country or colony. They make foreign goods more expensive to buy and provide funds for government operations.

Temperance Abstaining from the use of alcohol.

Union The name given to the supporters of the North in the American Civil War. The Union side wanted to keep the United States together.

Index

Credits

Cover top: House of Commons; bottom left: Ken Straiton/firstlight.ca; bottom right: CP/Ron Poling; Page 1 Courtesy Rogers Communications Inc.; Page 2 top left: map, Paperglyphs; top right: The Granger Collection; bottom: House of Commons; Page 3 Library and Archives Canada, C-006513; Page 4 The Granger Collection; Page 5 Charles William Jefferys, *Rebels of 1837 Drilling in North York*, 1898, Art Gallery of Ontario; Page 6 Ken Straiton/firstlight.ca; Page 7 map, Paperglyphs; Page 8 top: Library and Archives Canada, C-026348k; bottom: Mary Evans Picture Library; Page 9 top: Library and Archives Canada, C-047354; bottom: Library and Archives Canada, C-010103; Page 10 top: Mary Evans Picture Library; bottom: Courtesy of Steve Taylor and Views of the Famine; Page 11 left: © Bettmann/CORBIS; right: CBC, *Canada: A People's History*; Page 12 top: The Granger Collection; bottom: map, Paperglyphs; Page 13 top: Library and Archives Canada, C-029977; middle: The Granger Collection; bottom: The Granger Collection; Page 14 Library and Archives Canada, C-003371k; Page 15 top: Library and Archives Canada, e-000996469; bottom: Nova Scotia Museum History Collection; Page 16 top: McCord Museum of Canadian History; bottom: map, Paperglyphs; Page 17 top: McCord Museum of Canadian History; bottom: Library and Archives Canada, C-040148; Page 18 top: Glenbow Archives NA-325-4; bottom: Library and Archives Canada, C-114507; Page 19 Newberry Library, Chicago; Page 21 map, Paperglyphs; Page 22 Canadian Heritage Gallery; Page 24 John Gast, *American Progress*, 1872, Library of Congress; Page 26 top left: Library and Archives Canada, C-002162; bottom right: Library and Archives Canada, C-006513; right: Library and Archives Canada, C-009553; Page 27 left: Library

and Archives Canada, C-015369k; right: CBC, *Canada: A People's History*; Page 29 Library and Archives Canada, PA-091061; Page 30 Courtesy Rogers Communications Inc.; Page 32 Library and Archives Canada, C-000733; Page 34 Library and Archives Canada, C-095155; Page 36 Province House Ball, DH.83.65.1, Artist Dusan Kadlec, 8Parks Canada; Page 37 McCord Museum of Canadian History; Page 39 Library and Archives Canada, C-021604; Page 40 McCord Museum of Canadian History; Page 41 Library and Archives Canada, A-012632; Page 42 Library and Archives Canada, C-011351; Page 43 Library and Archives Canada, E-000009318; Page 45 Provincial Archives of Nfld. and Labrador; Page 46 Library and Archives Canada, C-041086k; Page 48 Library and Archives Canada, PA-025486; Page 49 top: McCord Museum of Canadian History; bottom: Library and Archives Canada, C-078761; Page 50 CBC, *Canada: A People's History*; Page 51 Library and Archives Canada, C-018737; Page 52 Library and Archives Canada, C-010109; Page 53 Courtesy of Rogers Communications Inc.; Page 54 from left to right: Library and Archives Canada, PA-033465; McCord Museum of Canadian History; Anne Nelson and Maggie, Ontario Legislative Library print collection, F2171-0-0-0-12, Archives of Ontario; CP/Ottawa Citizen/Chris Mikula; Illustrated News Library of Canada, 56366; Page 57 top: Library and Archives Canada, C-009480; bottom: Toronto Public Library Archives; Page 59 map, Paperglyphs; Page 60 top left: Library and Archives Canada, C-002500k, bottom left: CP; bottom right: fotosearch.com; Page 61 top left: Ken Straiton/firstlight.ca; top right: CP/Ron Poling; bottom: CP/Ryan Remiorz; Page 62 top: © Steven Croft/Masterfile; bottom: CP/Kevin Frayer; Page 63 CP/Ron Poling; Page 64 Library and Archives Canada, C-002500k.

Reviewers

Kathryn Brownell, Terry Fox School, Toronto, Ontario

Manny Calisto, West St. Paul School, West St. Paul, Manitoba

Greer Coe, Montague Intermediate School, Montague, Prince Edward Island

Rick Elliott, John Buchan School, Toronto, Ontario

Sheri Epstein, Langstaff High School, Thornhill, Ontario

Christine Greene, Avalon East School Board, St. John's, Newfoundland

Joanne Wheeler, St. Margaret School, Calgary, Alberta